Sundays
+ OTHER MUSINGS

Sundays
+ OTHER MUSINGS

Notes on Living Well
by Brandie Freely

LUMIN PUBLISHING HOUSE
Los Angeles, California

Sundays + Other Musings
Copyright © 2025 Brandie Freely
ISBN: 979-8-218-59838-9

Published by LUMIN Publishing House
Los Angeles, California

First Edition, 2025
Second Printing, 2025

All rights reserved. No part of this book may be reproduced in any form without prior written permission from the author and publisher. Please email bfree@brandiefreely.com for permission requests, special orders, author or publisher information.

Cover design: Brandie Freely & Emily Anne Evans
Typesetting: Emily Anne Evans

For my parents.

Mama, you never missed any of it, and that mattered to me. Thank you.
Daddy, for ensuring that the promise over your life extended to me.
I love you both. Your prayers are still carrying and covering me.

For Arnold.

You've been the wind beneath my wings, and it has meant the world to me. May your ROI take you even higher and cause you to soar.

For my babies, Solona and Lenox.

I write so that you can always hear Mommy's voice. Know that everything I do is with you in mind. I hope I have shown you what it means to be free and belong to yourself, first. This is your life. Make it beautiful and wonder-full. I love you more than the most perfect words could ever express.

"Sundays have always been our one true constant."
— *my mama, Tammie Terrell*

Spring 3

Summer 73

Fall 135

Winter 197

Author's Note

I can't say for sure I've always loved Sundays the way I do now. I can certainly recall the countless Sunday mornings I dreaded what the day would bring: wearing uncomfortable dresses I didn't even like to church for what felt like the entire day long.

That was early on. At some point I came to understand that the ritual of Sunday felt good. To engage in a practice that fed the soul came to feel right. Sunday became a refuge. A sanctuary. A place where burdens could be laid down and spirits could be lifted.

I grew up a church girl. Very much so. Understand. The Southern Baptist Black Church is its own culture. Its own denomination if you will. I'm laughing now as I remember. Time spent in those spaces with those people are some of the best memories of my life. And now tears are welling in my eyes. The community. My God, so rich. So significant to my formation. That kind of anchor. That sort of knowing. There's just nothing I can really compare it to; I just know that to have had it is extraordinary.

As a grown woman, now with my own family and my own life experiences, my Sunday practice looks different. It has looked different in various seasons of my life. And I find that to be okay. The roots are there. The anchor is still in place. And that has allowed me to expand and explore and be curious and open – all while remaining grounded in my personal truths.

What has remained is the sense of coming home I feel on Sundays. It's almost like during the week I'm out hunting and foraging and focusing on survival. And when Sunday comes, I get to return home to myself. I get to lay down and rest. And breathe and reset.

I get to take a look around me and notice all the things I didn't see when I was busy out in the world. I can take my time and really see. And the gratitude I feel when I do? Ah. Yes. I wish I could stay in that feeling, you know what I mean?

And so that's how this book came to be. I began writing about my love for Sundays and sharing it with my online community some time ago. And every time I did it would resonate with thousands of people. I love that Sunday feels like home to so many of us, and it is a pleasure putting into words what so many of us feel about it.

It must be said that for some, Sunday looks different. Maybe your rest and return home to yourself is on a Saturday (The Sabbath for many) or on a Monday (your day off from work). *Sunday* is my sacred day, and that is what this book is dedicated to: the sacredness of *Sunday* in my life. You can replace it for whatever your sacred day might be.

This book means we can take *Sunday* wherever we go. We can open *Sundays + Other Musings* up to any page, and there *Sunday* is. That feeling, that reset, that home-ness, that knowing, that anchor, that refuge, that sanctuary – all right there on the pages. Reminders, affirmations, good feelings and memories, spirit lifting and soul-feeding, joy and hope and love.

May you find what you need when you need it – on these pages and in your whole life.

May God bless and keep you.

And may everyday feel something like a Sunday.

With a Sunday kind of love,
b

Sundays
IN SPRING

Spring gives us so much reason to believe in life and lean into it. That the days go from mostly gray to an explosion of fresh, vibrant colors is not a thing we should just look past. It turns. The colors. The seasons. The tide. Yeah? The day. The circumstances. The weather. It goes from cold to warm. The days go from feeling cut short to once again granting us more time in the daylight. It all turns. It all changes all the time. And that is something we can depend on.

And so when spring gifts us all with its colors – hues of green, pink and periwinkle and lively yellows and tangerines – we must notice.

Spring reminds us that we can always count on life to bloom again. And that it will always gift us some color sometime.

Oh, to wake up on Sunday.
Everything made new. Again.

Sundays are for softness.

Author's Note:

And what even is softness? For me, it is ease above all.
It is moving through life gently and unhurried.
I am soft with myself, especially, and I extend that softness
to others as well. Softness is about intentionally
seeking out the beautiful and moving through life in a way that
feels light and gracious.
Maybe softness is what perpetual self-forgiveness feels like.

Sunday

is my

(self) love

language.

Sundays are for lovers of:

self.

life.

joy.

light.

goodness.

love.

Sunday,

I love waking up to the softness of you. Gentle mornings, quiet and slow, are my favorite. After a week of facing the unknown, you are sure. I'm sure I can rest on Sunday. I'm sure I can take it easy. I'm sure I can reset and find a reason to try again. I'm sure I'll be able to find some hope somehow. I'm sure I'll breathe more intentionally and feel a little more life in my body. On Sunday, I'm sure I will be okay.

And that is why you're my favorite, Sunday. You're like a little booster shot to my belief. You give me strength to keep going. At least until another Sunday comes around.

On Sundays my heart is wide open.

Open to ease.

Open to surrender.

Open to forgiveness.

Open to love.

Open to rest.

Open to softness.

Open to peace.

Open to joy.

Open to grace.

Open to abundance.

Open to believing that I'm even worthy of any of it at all.

Sunday Affirmations:

It will all be okay.

I will keep my mind and remain centered and calm no matter what.

There is always, always hope.

Love is still the right answer.

I am safe and covered and kept.

I can do hard things.

And I can also allow and accept when things come with ease.

My life is good, and I will let it be.

I am open to all the ways life wants to pour into me and fill my cup.

I can expect an overflow of goodness in my life.

Even me.

SUNDAYS IN SPRING

Sundays are for leaning into
the way we want our life to feel.

On My Mama.

I was just sitting here asking myself
what season reminds me of my mama?
And now I'm wondering what season reminds you of yours.
And which one reminds my mama of her mama.

Truth is, my mama can fit perfectly into any of the seasons. She's that kinda girl. Put her anywhere, and she will immediately belong. You know what I mean? People love her, and they love having her around. She has the kind of smile that starts in the corners of her eyes, so you know it's real. That's my favorite thing about her. She is electric, really. A lot like Summer. She has a zest for life, I love to say. She'll make you want to live like that. Full of life and optimism and joy and pure goodness.

She reminds me of Fall, too, the way she's willing to let go and get in the wind. My mama is who showed me what it meant to be free. She would leave us with her husband, my daddy, and fly overseas to live her life and pursue her dreams. I don't remember the few days long stints she'd be gone, and I don't remember how she managed to also never miss one, single event or school show – but I do remember wanting to be just like her. I am my mother's daughter.

Winter also reminds me of my mama. Because although I'm in my forties, hers are still the arms that offer the most warmth and comfort when the days are cold. To lay in her lap. To have her play in my hair. To have my mama wipe my tears away. To see that it's going to be okay when her eyes smile at me. I still and always will need my mama. A home cooked meal from her. Nourishment. Nurturing. Care. You know what I mean? A quiet retreat; my mama's arms. Real rest.

And well, to know my mama is to know she can and will name every single flower she passes by. She embodies Spring. She really does. The colors. Life. Newness. Face to the sun. Swaying in the wind. Roots deep. My mama is the most beautiful wildflower I've ever seen. I'm so grateful to come from her. She's got the greenest thumb. I used to think I didn't inherit it. That it must've skipped me. And that maybe, hopefully, at least my daughter would get it.

And then one day I realized I just had to learn to see God in flowers, the way she does. The colors, textures, shapes and fragrances just needed to blow my mind – and then I'd learn to keep them alive.

I'm so glad I have my mama's eyes. The kind of eyes that can see God in every detail.
I'm so glad she helped me see the beauty in every season.
I'm so glad to be her only girl.
So glad to be the seed of such a rare and beautiful and ever-blooming wildflower.

BRANDIE FREELY

I wouldn't take even one drop of rain
away from my life.
I absolutely love
the way I've bloomed.

Lean all the way into the good of your life.

On Sundays, we exhale the heaviness of the
week prior. On an inhale, we extend our arms
so that our chest stretches out and
upward.
Centered again, we lift our face to
the light.
And we re-open our heart.
Exhale again.
We let go.

As I open
up to life,
it opens
up to me.

Sundays are sweet reminders that
we can always begin again.

Gratitude

And what is simply taking one moment out of an entire day to notice the good?

Well, it is everything.

A Mindful Granola Situation

One of the ways I ground and slow down is to practice mindfulness through food: prepping (chopping, mixing, etc.), cooking, baking and of course savoring it in the end.

Something I really enjoy making is granola. Here, I'm sharing a recipe and way for you to make it mindfully when you have the time and space.

What you'll need:

- 3 cups rolled oats
- 1/2 cup nuts (almonds, pecans or walnuts)
- 1/4 cup seeds (sunflower, pumpkin or chia)
- 1/2 teaspoon cinnamon
- 1/4 cup melted coconut or olive oil
- 1/3 cup honey or maple syrup
- 1 teaspoon vanilla extract
- A pinch of sea salt
- Optional: 1/2 cup dried fruit (raisins, cranberries or apricots)

What you'll do:

1. **Prepare the Space:** Start by setting up your space with intention. Clear your kitchen area, ensuring it feels open and inviting. Take a deep breath, appreciating the time you're giving yourself to create something nourishing.

2. **Preheat the Oven:** Preheat your oven to 325°F. Consider the warmth of your home. Allow thoughts of gratitude to enter your heart and mind.

3. **Mix the Dry Ingredients:** In a large (pretty) bowl, combine the oats, nuts, seeds, cinnamon and salt. As you mix, engage your senses fully. Feel the texture of the oats and the nuts in your hands, listen to the sound they make as you mix, and notice the scent of cinnamon filling the air. Take time to appreciate each ingredient and how they contribute to the final creation.

4. **Create the Liquid Mixture:** In a smaller bowl, whisk together the melted coconut oil, honey (or maple syrup) and vanilla extract. As you whisk, focus on the rhythm of your hand and the way the ingredients come together into a smooth blend. Let it be a gentle reminder that even small actions, like stirring, can bring joy.

5. **Combine and Coat:** Pour the liquid mixture over the dry ingredients. As you combine them, use your hands or a wooden spoon, moving slowly and deliberately. Imagine yourself infusing love and care into the granola as you mix everything evenly, ensuring each oat and nut is well-coated. Feel connected to the act of nourishing your body.

6. **Spread and Bake:** Spread the granola mixture onto a lined baking sheet (I use parchment paper). Take a moment to make the layer even, smoothing it out mindfully. Slide the tray into the oven and set the timer for 20-25 minutes.

7. **Mindfully Check and Stir:** Halfway through the baking process, gently stir the granola to ensure it cooks evenly. As you open the oven, inhale the warm, comforting aroma, allowing it to bring you into the present.

8. **Cool and Add Dried Fruit:** Once the granola is golden and crisp, remove it from the oven and let it cool. As it cools, feel free to add dried fruit if desired. Take in the colors and textures as you mix them into the granola, once again moving mindfully and slowly.

9. **Serve and Savor:** When the granola is cool, serve yourself a small bowl.* Eat slowly, savoring each bite. Notice the crunch, the sweetness, and the satisfaction it brings to your body.

* I personally love to eat my granola with yogurt and/or oatmeal.

On Sundays, I do maintenance on my nervous system.

Author's Note:

Just like we schedule maintenance on our cars and homes
and teeth and hair, I do a regular assessment of my body's
communication network, my nervous system.
I check in to ensure that I'm able to shift
from go mode to rest mode smoothly, with no glitches.
Sundays signal to my brain, and my brain signals my body:
Breathe. You're safe here.

SUNDAYS IN SPRING

On Sundays I work on soul things,
like grounding and gratitude and breathing
and not rushing. Like being present and not
being anxious. Like forgiving myself and
accepting whatever is – while making room
for whatever might be.

BRANDIE FREELY

My body responds to Sundays.
It's like it unwinds itself
and releases into
a sweet surrender.

I am not required
to hold it all together.
I can let go over and over again.

Sunday,

You remind me that I have access to an endless Source: A Source of strength. Of peace that surpasses my understanding. Of joy. Of help. Of living water that won't run dry. Yes, you do, Sunday. You remind me of God things. You remind me to look up and notice how beautiful it all is. Life. Love. Family. Home. You slow me down enough to see it all and appreciate it. Thank you for reminding me that time is of the essence. And paying attention to it is an art. I love making it back to you, Sunday. You really do have my heart.

Sunday Affirmations:

I am entering a season of abundance.

No good thing is being withheld from me.

God is sending a fresh wind my way.

My life is on the right track.

Everything is aligning in my favor, even now.

I believe in miracles because my life is one.

Anything is possible.

God can turn it around. Whatever it is.

I am blessed.

I am not forgotten.

My life is a sure thing; not a maybe kinda thing.

I know who I am.

I am loved.

On Sundays
I feel brand new like the morning.

That good feeling you feel on Sundays –
take it everywhere.
Take Sunday wherever you go.

Sunday Mornings at the Farmer's Market

One of my favorite things to do on a Sunday morning is get up early, throw on something California cute and head to the Farmer's Market. For me, it's the whole entire experience. It's the drive down Ocean Avenue right alongside the Pacific Ocean. It's the palm trees dancing through my sunroof along the way. It's the groups of bikers I pass by, out in the early hours of the day doing what they love. It's the smiling faces and Sunday morning perkiness that greet me when I arrive. Morning people are delightful. Did you know that? I think they must just automatically feel better about themselves for having gotten ahead of the day. You know? That's how rising early makes me feel, anyway.

I love the energy exchange as we shop and chat about our produce and locally sourced foods for the week. Ah. And I love talking to the farmers. I ask all the questions about even the things I think I know:

Q: *What's the best way to preserve my plums?*
A: (from one of the veteran vendors there; a woman): *Don't stack them. Lay them side by side, and let them breathe. And the unripe ones? Put 'em in the fridge, and then take 'em out a day or two before you want to eat them. Be sure to eat the ripe ones now.*

I get so much satisfaction from these Sunday learnings. I have so much gratitude and awe perusing the booths and admiring the rich colors, the shapes and sizes, the health benefits, science and uses behind the various fruits, vegetables, grains, oats, etc.

And I have so much respect for the farmers. Their hands, their backs, their diligence, their knowledge, their humility, their genius, their intune-ness with the earth, and Mother Nature and God. *What, on Earth, would we do without them?*

Sunday feels like a warm embrace that squeezes life and love into the parts of me that need it most.

Be careful not to miss out on the good of your life always searching for the better.

There's no nap quite like a Sunday afternoon nap.

Author's Note:

I grew up in the kind of neighborhood you don't really hear
much about. First of all, my dad built most of the houses in it.
My neighbors were Black, home-owning families
with two parents raising their Black children. Everyone lived on an acre of land.
And we shared all the yards. There were no fences. We basically all lived together,
all the kids. My little brother would be up and down the street barefoot.
My older brother was breaking basketball goals along with the other
big guys playing 21. It was one long street that looped in the back.
 Landmark. That was its name.
My grandpa lived there. My uncle, my daddy's brother. My grandmothers (both)
lived on that street at one point in time.
Next door to our home lived my second family.
I love them so. A day in my life looked like going to school,
 getting home, walking across the yard,
walking through their back door (no knock).
Checking to see what was being whipped up in the kitchen, a gumbo
or maybe a coconut meringue pie (from scratch).
And then laying down in my favorite spot on the couch.
It was like a Sunday nap every day of the week.
A beautiful blessing.
The kind of beauty that shaped how I see the world and its possibilities.

Sundays gift me another chance.

I handle it with care.

In the Light

May I always be in the light
or headed towards it.
May I know the way the light feels
on my skin so that even when it is dark,
I can sense it.
And may I be so electric,
so full of light
that I am able to transfer energy
to others
and still never run out.
May it be so that if I am light,
those around me can't help but be
illuminated, too.

May I be a light source.

Blessed and kept.

May my cup remain so full
that I am an endless resource for those
who need to be poured into.

Sunday Affirmations:

What's for me is for me.

What's mine is mine.

The only difference between those
who do and those who don't is that
one kept going while the other gave in.

I am getting where I'm going.

I trust the timing of my life.

My life is good, because I say it is.

I am careful with myself.

I take good care of me.

May the fragrance of my life
be the kind that is sweet
and lingers on everything
it touches.

My Uncle Reggie's Banana Pudding

My uncle's love for being in the kitchen makes me feel connected to my grandparents. I was young when PawPaw passed, about fifth or sixth grade, so I can't remember everything in as much detail as I'd like. What I do remember is that he was always in the kitchen. Sometimes I'd come home from school and there he was making his Terrell Special or some other delicious dish we'd have for dinner. PawPaw lived across the street from us. Uncle Reggie lived next door. And for a while Grandma (her and PawPaw weren't together anymore) lived in the garage apartment just outside our back door. Grandma was a baker, a gardener and herbalist. She'd take me on walks up to the gigantic pecan tree at the front of our street, and we'd collect the good ones. Then she'd bake a pie.

And I just wish I understood how precious that time was, you know? With both of them. What I wouldn't do to go back and just soak up as much of my loved ones as humanly possible. You just don't realize how profoundly you'll miss something while you still have it. There's just no way to know.

Banana Pudding reminds me of home. Sundays. Family. Family dinners. Precious time spent. When I was leaving Texas in 2017, Uncle Reggie sent me with a huge bowl of it to keep in the cooler for the long road trip. And every time I've returned home since, he's made it for me.

When I asked him if I could add his recipe to this book he said *I mean, there's nothing special about it.*

Except there is something so special. *There's the time we'll get to spend together here in this kitchen. Time that I know is precious.*

What you'll need:

- 3/4 cup granulated sugar, divided
- 1/3 cup all-purpose flour
- Dash of salt
  (for balance)
- 3 large eggs, separated
  (room temperature for easier separation)
- 2 cups milk
  (whole milk for richness works best)
- 1/2 teaspoon pure vanilla extract
  (a comforting finish)
- About a 1/2 box of Nilla Wafers
  (or Chessman Cookies if you're feeling fancy)
- About 5 ripe bananas, sliced

What you'll do:

1. **Prepare your double boiler:** Set a heatproof bowl over a saucepan of simmering water, ensuring the bottom of the bowl doesn't touch the water. This gentle method prevents burning.

2. **Separate the eggs:** Bring your eggs to room temperature first; they separate more easily this way. Carefully separate yolks from whites, placing yolks in a medium bowl and whites in another (if you'd like to make a meringue topping later).

3. **Make the pudding base:** In your double boiler, combine ½ cup of the sugar, your flour and the pinch of salt. Stir in the egg yolks and milk. Cook over medium heat. You'll want to stand right near your mixture, stirring constantly, until the mixture thickens. It should be able to coat the back of a spoon without running off, and that's how you'll know it's thick enough. Remove from heat and then stir in the vanilla extract.

4. **Layer your pudding:** Begin your layering in a casserole dish or pretty serving bowl. Start with Nilla Wafers or Chessman Cookies on the bottom, followed by a layer of sliced bananas. The ratio of cookies to bananas comes down to personal preference – use more bananas for a fruit-forward dessert, or more cookies for a sturdier texture. Repeat the layering until all your ingredients are used.

5. **Now. Pour and settle:** Gently pour the warm pudding over the layered cookies and bananas, ensuring everything is evenly coated. Let it sit briefly, allowing the pudding to soak into the cookies and meld with the bananas.

6. **Cool and enjoy:** Allow the pudding to cool slightly before serving warm,* or refrigerate if you prefer a chilled dessert.

Optional meringue topping:

7. Preheat your oven to 350°F.

8. Whisk the reserved egg whites with the remaining ¼ cup sugar until stiff peaks form. Spread over the pudding, creating soft swirls and peaks with your spoon.

9. Place the dish in the oven and bake for 10-15 minutes, or until the meringue is golden.

* *My dad and uncle both prefer their banana pudding warmed, so they'll put it in the microwave for a few seconds before enjoying it. I've never tried it. You?*

I've come to realize that my love for Sundays
is rooted in the practice of gratitude.
Of all the days, on Sundays, I remember
to notice just how blessed my life
really is.

SUNDAYS IN SPRING

I'm adorable at fresh starts, and that's why Sundays look so good on me.

A Sunday Prayer:

May you give yourself what you need this week. May you listen inward to what your body and spirit are asking of you. May you go easy on yourself and take your precious time. No anxiety this week. Only deep breaths full of intention and confidence. May you trust that everything is unfolding just as it should. And may everything that has been getting you down begin to shift and even turn out better than you could've ever imagined. May you lean in and trust the process more this week. May those limiting beliefs be quiet in your mind. You can do whatever you set your mind and heart to. Believe that. Know that.

I hope it feels like Sunday anytime I'm around:
good vibes. ease. refreshing. don't want
it to end. joy. peace. beauty.
fun. freedom. love.

And in this short life, it is not
the letting go of a thing that I am fearful of;
it is the holding on for too long
that terrifies me.

Outer Space

The sound of the collision
is deafening
Reason cannot be heard
over the crash of feeling
Even the wind is shaken to stillness
and watches
as
light explodes
along with my heart
For a moment
there is only
a big bang
and this is my theory of you

Dear Sunday, fill me again. My empty places.
Please. Pour into me until I overflow.

A beautiful Sunday is soul medicine.

Don't believe the lies you tell yourself
when you're exhausted of it all.

The Art of Savoring

Sundays are for slowing down and savoring – not just the food on our plates but the moments of stillness we so rarely allow ourselves when we're in the rush of life. Cooking can become a meditative act when we approach it mindfully. Feel the textures beneath your fingers as you wash, chop and stir. Inhale the aroma of fresh herbs or roasting vegetables. Allow yourself to be fully present in the creation of your meal, honoring the nourishment you are preparing for your body and soul.

As you sit down to your Sunday dinner, why not set an intentional atmosphere. Lay the table as though you are dining with royalty – why not take yourself that seriously?

Light a candle, play soft music or sit outdoors and feel the breeze on your skin. Take a breath before your first bite. Let this meal be a reminder of the beauty of slowing down and being fully present.

Sundays are for romance.

Author's Note:

Romance really is about noticing how good something feels.
You know? Like being especially aware of the
sensations in our bodies and the emotions we're experiencing.
Real romance really comes down to paying attention.
Sundays are for that. For paying attention to how good life feels.

I love to romanticize my Sundays with fresh flowers,
a little Bossa Nova and baking when I can.
I like Sunday to feel soft and loving.
Like it knows me well.
And loves having me over.

God,
bless the man who chooses
to love her
despite her battle wounds
and please
help her
let him.

There is a garden

I must tend

and it is

my own.

May the sunlight reach you
wherever you are.
May it seep through every crack
and round every corner
just to touch your face.

Thing is, any time I've ever made it
to the other side of anything,
the grass has always been greener.

Sunday Affirmations:

I can sit in my joy; I don't need to rush out.

Peace is the tone of my whole life.

I will find peace no matter where I wander.

Love is always on its way to me.

The love in my life is abundant.

The joy in my life is abundant; I can always find it.

There is a lot of beauty in my life – I will remember to notice.

I am mastering faith and trust (belief and confidence) every day.

Everything is alright.

I am okay.

God is good.

BRANDIE FREELY

I like to use Sunday to count up all my blessings.

All week long I look forward to Sunday.
I know how it will make me feel. I am sure. Confident.
Certain. See. There's an intention there.
An expectation rooted in my trust and knowing.
And Sunday always delivers.

    Author's Note:

    The moral is that it matters when you expect good things.

How to have a soft Sunday

Sundays offer us a beautiful opportunity to not only reflect on the week that's passed but to also set gentle intentions for the days ahead. Planning your week doesn't have to be rigid or overwhelming – it can be a sacred act of self-love and care, where you create space for the things that nourish you, while still leaving room for spontaneity and flow.

Here's a simple suggestion to help you plan your week with softness and intention, making room for both productivity and peace. I do believe in spending some time reflecting and planning. When I do this, it always makes such a huge difference in the flow of things. You know?

1. **Reflect on the Previous Week**

    Before you begin planning for the upcoming week, take a few minutes to reflect on the one that has passed. Ask yourself:

    - What went well last week?
    - What moments felt particularly nourishing or fulfilling?
    - Where did I feel stressed or overwhelmed?

    By acknowledging the highs and lows of your week, you can approach the new one with clarity. Use this reflection as a guide to identify what you'd like to carry forward and what you want to leave behind.

2. **Prioritize Your Non-Negotiables**

   Start by identifying the top 2-3 things that truly matter to you this week. These might be work commitments, family obligations or personal care practices. Instead of overwhelming yourself with a long to-do list, focus on these key priorities. Keep it simple and gentle – less is more.

   Soft Tip: For every task you add, also schedule a moment of rest. For example, after a busy workday, plan a 15-minute break to sip tea, stretch or sit outside. This helps create balance and prevents burnout.

3. **Leave Space for Flexibility**

   While it's sweet to have a plan, give yourself permission to leave some space in your schedule for spontaneity or changes (we'll call it that vs "things not going according to plan"). A gentle week isn't overly packed or rigid. By allowing some flexibility, you give yourself room to flow with the unexpected – whether that's an opportunity to rest, play or shift priorities as needed.

   Soft Tip: A gentle reminder that you can erase things you wrote and even draw a line through them. A gentle reminder that things can be changed or moved. You know? *Let go of perfectionism and flow with the week.*

4. **Set Small, Joyful Intentions**

    In addition to your non-negotiables, ask yourself: "What would make me feel more joyful and peaceful this week?" This could be something as simple as taking a walk in nature, reading a chapter of a book or cooking a meal you love. Add these moments of joy into your schedule, just like you would any other task. They don't need to be grand, just intentional pockets of joy.

    Soft Tip: Plan a "mid-week pause" – a moment around Wednesday where you check in with yourself. Reassess how your week is going and see if you need to slow down, add more joy or adjust your priorities.

5. **Create Gentle Evening Rituals**

    Think about how you want to end your days during the week. Plan evening rituals and routines that allow you to unwind and reflect on the day. This might include journaling, a cup of calming tea, a skincare routine or even five minutes of mindful breathing before bed. Just 5 minutes. *We can do this!*

6. **Visualize a Week in Alignment**

    Close your Sunday planning by visualizing your week ahead, not just as a series of tasks, but as an experience. How do you want to feel each day? Visualize yourself moving through the week with grace, feeling grounded and supported. This gentle visualization sets a positive tone for the week to come, reinforcing that you are in alignment with your intentions and desires.

Softly into the week you go.

Sundays
IN SUMMER

Summer reminds us that life is for the living. Most things come fully alive in the summertime. Everything is illuminated, including us, revealing the richness and fullness of our truest colors.

Revealing who we are when we're free. Who we are when we seek and find adventure. Who we are when joy abounds.

Warmth on our skin, summer just *feels* good.

BRANDIE FREELY

Sunday stops by to remind us that we are free, indeed.

Author's Note:

I love having a choice. It is an extremely
underrated privilege, choice is. It's probably
because so often we find ourselves doing what we have
to do vs what we want to do. It's one of many reasons I love Sundays so much.
I wake up with choice at the forefront of my mind on Sunday – the way it
should be everyday.
How do I want to spend my precious time today?
How do I want it to *feel*?
And whatever I choose is okay.

On Sundays

I count it

all joy.

On Sundays I feel especially free and aware
of the vast possibilities of my life.
I feel like I can do anything or nothing at all.
And it will be beautiful either way.

On Sundays we lift our heads to the sun.

Close our eyes. And let it recharge us.

Fill us again.

My Daddy + Humanity

It occurred to me one day – and I'm so glad it did – that my dad is the first human being who introduced me to the concept of radical acceptance. Of course, I wasn't aware at the time, and neither was he. But I can certainly remember adopting the practice early on.

It's how I coped.

Growing up, my dad wasn't a lot of the things I believed I wanted, but he was everything I have ever needed. And so much more, really. Raising my own kids now, I can see (even more so) how much of parenting is just doing the best you can.

My dad taught me what it meant to have compassion for someone. And what it meant to trust a person's good intentions. See the good in them despite the not so good. You know what I mean?

He is the reason I study human nature; he's the source of my fascination. He's why I pay attention to all of it. Every part of what we (as humans, being) are. And what we do. And why.

See, I had to find a way to understand my dad. I had to care about his why. His own backstory. What he may have been lacking. I had to, because it helped prevent me from being too sad to care about myself. You understand?

I had to grasp the reality that we are still only ever human even on our best day. We're full of complexities and flaws and questions that have limited answers. We really all are a mystery seeking to be solved, aren't we?

I had to learn to understand us – humanity – because if I didn't, maybe the lack of the things I wanted, not necessarily needed, would have taken me out. Maybe I would've lost my human mind when it became too heavy, too hard to keep imagining or hoping for a different kind of life than the one I had.

I thank my daddy for the ability to understand beyond my limited perspective and feelings. For my ability to look at a thing for what it clearly is and also for what else it might be underneath. I thank him for teaching me to find the good in all things. To trust that it is always there somewhere. We'll likely never have this conversation. And that's a part of the things I want but don't need. But I'm sure in his own way, he understands me like I understand him.

Don't rush your life.

It goes on anyway.

Take your precious time.

All of it.

On Sundays I'm reminded of that ol' time phrase:

God has never failed me yet.

Found.

I know it's hard to hold onto something you can't see.
I know there are things you just don't understand. I know.
I know hope can be hard to find. I've been looking for it myself.
I've been wondering: where are you, Hope?
I can't see you. I'm having a hard time feeling you. I'm trying to hold onto you. Do you even want me to?

I look for hope again. Nothing. Silence.
And then.

After some time passes, and I resolve to stop looking.
Stop trying so hard because I'm tired. Stop overthinking.
Stop trying to understand because I can't. Then.
And only then.

Do I realize that hope never needed me to find it.
Hope is never the one who is lost.

And whenever I surrender.
Whenever I relax my worrisome brow. Whenever I just breathe.
And let go.
There is hope.
Right there all along.

It takes time to get it all together.

Sunday Affirmations:

Whatever I have needed, God has provided.

The above will never change.

I deserve to experience the goodness this life has to offer.

I am worthy.

If I have the courage to ask and believe, it is mine.

I have what it takes to respond to the call on my life.

I have purpose.

My life has meaning.

I am needed.

I am loved.

I am here.

Send your love. Shine your light.
Assert your influence. Be who you know
you are. Don't be afraid
of who you know you are. Do not dim.
Be so full of electricity, that darkness
could never consume you. Only light.
Only light.
Only light.

I am my favorite version of myself on any given Sunday:
Soft, surrendered, simplistic, still and settled in my spirit.

On Sundays I gladly exhale my burdens and inhale my blessings.

On Sundays

I lift my head

to *the sun.*

Sundays are for soft landings and gentle relaunches.

On Sundays I'm reminded of life's sweetness.

An Ode to My Ole Girl.

My best friend of twenty+ years and I love to talk like two very seasoned Southern women. We make sure our words and inflections drag so they're heard and felt. We communicate in the phrases our grandmothers did. It's our favorite thing to do and favorite way to be with one another.

I think we do it because it feels like warmth and wisdom. A loving hug and a knowing nod. It feels like big love that is somehow quiet and automatic. And that's exactly the way we are. We use a lot of words, but we don't need 'em.

Chile, we know what we sayin' without sayin' a thang at all. That's how best friends 'posed to be. Like two people who keep gettin' cut from the same cloth. Lifetime after lifetime after lifetime.

Ain't that a blessin'.

Ayron's Red Beans and Rice

My best friend is the type of person who was born knowing how to cook. Her food is an extension of her heart, and you can tell by how delicious it is. You know, the secret ingredient to food that touches your soul is *love*. Ask me how I know, and I'll go down the line of women in my life whose food fed more than just my physical. Each of them had a reverence for the way things should go in the kitchen. And if you didn't share the same respect, *out of my kitchen*, they'd order.

What you'll need:

- 1 bag dried red beans, soaked overnight (or at least a few hours)
- 1 yellow onion, chopped
- 1 green bell pepper, chopped
- 5-6 garlic cloves, minced
- 1 package smoked turkey tails (for that deep, rich flavor)
- 1 package Conecuh sausage, sliced (or any smoked or andouille sausage)
- 3 bay leaves
- Chicken stock (enough to cover the ingredients)
- Cajun seasoning, salt and black pepper (to taste)
- Knorr chicken bouillon, to taste
- Cooked white rice (for serving)
- Optional: diced raw onion for garnish (the real Southern way)

What you'll do:

1. **Soak the Beans:** Start by soaking your red beans overnight for the best texture, or for at least a few hours if time is tight. Drain and rinse when you're ready to cook.

2. **Brown the Sausage:** In a large, heavy-bottomed pot, sauté the sliced sausage over medium heat until browned and caramelized. Let the smoky aroma fill your kitchen, a reminder that this dish is as much about savoring the process as the result.

3. **Build Your Flavor Base:** Add the chopped onion, bell pepper and garlic to the pot. Sauté until softened, letting the "holy trinity" of Southern flavors come alive in the pot.

4. **Add the Turkey Tails:** Place the smoked turkey tails into the pot, layering in even more flavor. Trust the process – there's deep, delicious flavor waiting to be coaxed out of those tails.

5. **Add Stock and Season:** Pour enough chicken stock (or a mix of stock and water) to cover the turkey tails, then season to taste with Cajun seasoning, salt and black pepper. Add the bay leaves. Stir in a little Knorr chicken bouillon for that extra layer of flavor.

6. **Boil and Simmer:** Bring the mixture to a gentle boil over medium heat, letting it cook for about an hour. During this time, the turkey tails will release their flavor into the broth, setting a savory base for your beans.

7. **Add the Beans:** Add the soaked beans to the pot and check your seasonings. Add a little more if needed, but let the flavors continue to build slowly.

8. **Cook Low and Slow:** Reduce the heat to medium-low, allowing the beans to cook for 1-2 hours. Check on them every 30 minutes, stirring and adjusting the seasonings if needed, until the beans are soft and creamy.

9. **Shred the Turkey Meat:** Once the beans are tender, remove the turkey tails, shred the meat and return it to the pot. This step brings even more of that rich, smoky flavor into the soup.

10. **Mash and Thicken:** Take about a cup of beans from the pot and mash them with a spoon before stirring them back in. This thickens the broth, giving it that comforting, creamy texture. Let the pot simmer for another 30 minutes.

11. **Serve Over Rice:** Ladle the beans over a bed of warm white rice, letting each spoonful bring you into that slow, soul-satisfying rhythm. For a true Southern touch, sprinkle with diced raw onion before serving.

May I carry light.

Everywhere.

Everywhere.

All the time.

All the time.

Sunday,

We meet again, thank God. I've been needing the lightness you bring. The past week felt heavy, and I grew weary of carrying it on my mind. I've been looking forward to you and the sense of permission you give to lay it all down. Sunday, I'll have to hold you close this week and carry you wherever I go. So much is going on, and the outcome, I don't know. But. I am sure that some things always remain no matter how other things change. Like you, Sunday. You'll always be there to remind me of Amazing Grace.

On Sundays the delight I have in this life
is amplified.

Sunday Affirmations:

I *get to* be alive and create the life of my dreams.

I am allowed to get it wrong sometimes.

I can start over anytime.

I am getting where I'm going.

If it takes some time, that is okay. And I am okay.

I am working on my patience.

Trusting the process takes practice.

I am seen, known and loved by The Highest Source.

On Sundays I turn off autopilot.

Author's Note:

I really hate that it's true, but a lot of our precious
time is spent doing what we *always* do, which means
we're not really thinking about what we're doing, because we don't have to.
You know? We're simply moving through familiar motions.
And truly, our thoughts are everywhere *BUT* in the moment.
That is autopilot.
And that is what we do not do on Sundays, especially.
On Sundays we live, breathe and experience our being
with love and gratitude and intention and presence.

SUNDAYS IN SUMMER

Sundays are our favorite because at the core
of our being we crave simplicity and softness and ease.
We crave things that have meaning and add value to our lives.
Sundays do that. They add to us. They are good to us and for us.
We need Sundays.

Sundays make me feel like it's perfectly okay to start over – even from scratch.

My Favorite Sugar Cookies *From Scratch*

What you'll need:

- 2 soft sticks of butter
- 1 egg
  (a big one)
- 1 1/2 cups of granulated sugar
- 1/2 teaspoon of salt
- 1/2 teaspoon of baking powder
- 1 teaspoon of vanilla extract
- About 1/4 cup more of sugar for rolling the cookie dough

What you'll do:

1. Preheat oven to 350°F.
2. Drop softened butter sticks into the bowl of your mixer.
3. Cream it together with the sugar until fluffy. About 2-3 minutes.
4. Add your egg until everything is combined.
5. Mix in the rest of your dry ingredients.
6. Add vanilla.
7. Now scoop the dough by 1-2 tablespoons and roll into a ball.
8. On a flat surface (like a plate) pour and spread out the remaining sugar.
9. Roll each ball into the sugar to coat it before placing them on parchment paper on your baking sheet.
10. Place the cookies 1-2 inches apart and light press each one down with the back of a spoon.
11. Bake for 8-10 minutes or until light golden brown around the edges.

Stay open,
because
you
just never
know.

I adore Sundays, because I'm into fresh
starts. I'm big on newness, mercy, grace,
second chances, redos and undos
and things of the sort.

Sundays

are a balm

for the soul.

On Finding Your People:

How it works is: You show up as your most authentic self every single day,
no matter how hard. And you begin to see people fall off, maybe people you thought
really loved you. And it hurts, and you think about going back to pretending, but you don't.
And eventually, the right people begin showing up in your life.
People who love the real you. And they raise your vibrations, and you become lighter.
And higher. And better. Because no matter how convinced you are otherwise, you need people.
You need the right people – to get where you're going.
And that's how it works.

It's okay to long for love.

Means your heart still works.

Is ripe. Is ready.

May the sweetest love
be on its way
to you
right now.

Sundays are like a refill station for your journey.

Sunday Affirmations:

I am loved.

I am seen.

I am known.

I am shined upon.

I am healed.

I have joy.

I have peace.

I can let go.

I am safe.

It is working together for me.

Everything is alright.

I trust God.

And I surrender.

I'm squeezing all the juice out of this life.
You hear me?

Author's Note:

The secret of life is not only making lemonade out of lemons –
but it is *understanding* the benefits of the lemons.
It is looking into the countless ways lemons make us better.
Because listen.
If you can't understand the good of lemons, you'll be aggrieved,
squeezing out their juice.
It'll turn out bitter and you'll resent it – and also turn bitter.
But when you can appreciate the lemons, you'll find yourself
singing with spirit as you squeeze
and dancing in surrender as you stir.
Your lemonade will be sweetened with freedom, peace, gratitude,
love, understanding, and compassion.
Everyone will want you to pour into their cup.
And they'll want to know
how you sweetened that thang like that.
And it will bring you immeasurable joy to tell them.

SUNDAYS IN SUMMER

Sundays are for exhales and calmness and good thoughts and relaxed shoulders. And optimism. And hope. And love. And lightness. And joy. And gratitude. And peace. And beauty. And seeing the good.

Sundays bring out the best in me.

On Sunday,

Hey, listen to me. You can let all that stuff you're holding onto go. You can lay it all down. It's been heavy on you, hasn't it? And it was never even yours to carry.

It is enough just trying to be a good human and keep your mind. If you hold onto anything, let it be that. Let it be your mind and your beautiful heart. Start today with surrender. Release whatever weighs too much. Today is a good day to consider the wear and tear on your mental and your nervous system. It's a good day to care about healing.

On Love.

        The thing we're searching for through it all is love.
        Love me, will you?
        Just as I am, will you choose to see me and think I am beautiful this way?

        Especially as I'm changing. And especially if I change in a way you weren't expecting. Will you still choose to see that I am beautiful this way?

Ultimately, love is the thing we need most.
And in the same breath, it is the hardest thing to
find,
have
and keep.

We spend a significant portion of our lives searching for a love that will remain the same.
But love changes.
And it should be free to.

Love needs no ownership. Love just is.

Through tears in your eyes, can you still see that it's me?
And if your chest caves a little, can you remember how we were and that it was beautiful?
And that we are still beautiful how we are?

This world can't run at its full electric
capacity if you dim your light.
Do not rob us, please.
Turn your light up.
All the way. Thank you.

On Sundays I remember to show up for myself.

Sundays are built for ease and things that feel like the warmth of the sun.

People who love Sundays are my kind of people.

Worth it.

Staying in the light can come at a cost.
It can cost you forgiveness with no apology.
It can cost you being misunderstood by those you love.
It can cost you forgetting some good parts
if they are attached to some bad parts.
It can cost you loving people in spite of.
It can cost you boundaries, even distance.
It can cost you relationships that meant something to you.
It can cost you being labeled: delusional or a pretender.
It can cost you radical, unconditional acceptance.

But pay the cost anyway.

Because being a light is the reason we're even here.
And packing light is the only way
we should ever want to journey through this life.

I'll pay the cost everytime.
Just keep me where the light is.

SUNDAYS IN SUMMER

On Sundays I look into how my story is going and determine whether or not it's in need of some changes. If so, I simply begin a rewrite. And I love that for me.

Sunday Affirmations:

I deserve a life that is soft.

My life is meaningful and also fulfilling.

My life is wonder-full.

I am getting where I'm going.

No good thing will God withhold from me.

Everything that is meant for me will find its way to me.

I am right where I'm supposed to be.

My life is right on time.

I embrace the unknown.

I trust that the seasons know best when it's time to change.

I trust the process.

I'll take some rain with my sunshine.
It all works together.

Sunday,

I love how you bring me back to the start again. And give me another chance to get it right. No matter what happened all week long, high or low, you ground me right at my center again. Sunday, you fill my cup to the top. And you remind me that it's all okay. Thank you for being a constant. A place of refuge and revival for my fragile heart. I will love you forever for supplying me with what I need to keep showing up. And keep going.

On Sundays I sit in gratitude for all the good in my life. And while sitting, I also open myself wide enough to receive the abundance of the good that is still on its way to me.

Sonday

People often smile our way or stop us when we're out in public to talk about how adorable my son's love for his mama is. There were two memorable occasions in Trader Joe's when this happened.

One Sunday (because that's usually when I do my grocery run), he was sitting in the cart facing me. We were finding our way around the produce section, trying to navigate grocery store traffic when he decided it was the perfect time to reach for my face. Of course I leaned in to ask him what he needed, only for him to grab my entire head and pull me in for the biggest, slobberiest kiss. Right there in the middle of the store. He held me there for the longest time. To the point where people stood around laughing and watching his display of affection for me.

Another time an older lady seemed to be watching us as we circled the same produce section. She kept showing up in the section we were in and kind of inching her way closer. I smiled at her multiple times as our eyes continued to lock. Finally, she touched my arm to stop me and share a story.

Your son reminds me of my grandson. I remember attending a ballet with him and his mom. He was so obsessed with her. He held her close the entire night, leaning in for cuddles and kisses and just lavishing her with his love.

I always walk away from those encounters with a warm feeling of gratitude. That people look at my little brown boy and see love. That they see what he actually *is*. A boy with a heart of gold, sweet and kind. Helpful always. Smart and charming. Smiling and friendly. Always grabbing my hand to kiss it, or rubbing my back and feet (his daddy taught him well). He's so in love with me. He is my sonshine. Pure and sweet. Joy personified. I love him so, so much.

BRANDIE FREELY

I am
constantly
turning and
re-
turning
and re-
turning

and
returning
to myself.

I have to wake up every single day and let go again.
Every single day
I have to remember
to surrender.

And may Sundays feel like everything is brand new.

Fresh. Light. Burdens down.

Like you are loved. Seen. Known and forgiven.

Thought of. Considered. Kept.

Sunday Affirmations:

I have joy.

I have peace.

I am love. And I am loved.

I am light. And I move through my life that way.

I am finding my way.

I am not too late to my destination.

My journey is golden.

My unique lived experience is valuable.

There is enough resource in this world for me.

I am not forgotten.

Life is good.

God is good.

It is well in my soul.

Sundays
IN FALL

Fall is our favorite season for many reasons. There's its perfect weather – a reprieve from the heat of Summer. There's the slowing down and settling back into routines, which is more than welcomed after several months of being busy and on the go in Summer, trying to make the most of everyone's open schedules. There's the start of the holidays. They give us reason to tap into gratitude and meaning. But most of all, we love fall because it gives us permission to exhale and release what we are no longer able or willing to hold. Fall shows us how to let go. And it reminds us that there is beauty in releasing the old to make room for the new.

Sundays are for letting go
of whatever happened
prior to right now.

Let it fall away.

A picture of Sunday

I like to get outside early on a Sunday morning. Just after the sun comes up. I love to venture out and find my people. They're up, too. Some of them running or riding bikes on the path along the beach. Others practicing Tai Chi in the patches of grass under palm trees, where everything is always okay. I love that they, like me, arise and just want to be in the sun as much and as soon as possible. I'm usually passing by them around 7:30 AM at the latest, down Pacific Coast Highway, smiling, my windows cracked. The crisp air flowing in finds my grateful cheeks and reminds me that it is so, so sweet to be alive at all.

Bring back slow living.
Especially on Sundays.
It's just going too fast.
Everything.

Author's Note:

Sometimes I long for the slowness of life
we experienced during the pandemic. I love to call it
The Great Pause. That was when we fully
leaned into romanticizing the mundane.
That was when waiting for dough to rise and
the smell of freshly baked bread
and homemade pasta began to mean something
to me. That was when I realized just how
precious our time really is.

We don't just break for no reason.
We break open – to reveal ourselves.
And don't we want to be fully revealed?
Fully known? Fully ourselves?

In the Wind

Last night I dreamt
of a wildflower
She was swaying
on a vast field
in the wind, almost dancing
She was bending
and stretching herself
so beautifully

She even smiled at me
just when a rush blew in
causing all her petals to
gleam

I noticed she wasn't worried
that the ground beneath her
might let go
or that she might fly away
and lose herself

She was confident in her roots
so much so that

she could be herself:
wild
and free

I couldn't look away
She reminded me
of me

The way she adorned herself
with the light of the sun
and no matter how it blew
danced with the wind

She sang a song to me
it went:
remember who you are again

Sunday,

The past week broke my heart as some weeks do. It knocked the wind out of me, and I wondered if I would ever breathe the same again. I fear I'm holding my breath even now.

I know I have to keep breathing.
Exhale. I'm trying.
Inhale. I'm here.

Would you help me remember that it all works together for the greater good. Would you do that thing you do where you lift the heaviness of the week prior and send me on my way into the light-ness? Remind me again that I love to be in the light. That I'm not the kinda girl that carries all the loads and things. I lay that stuff down. And I surrender and trust. And I pick up hope. And peace. And joy. And love. The kind Sunday taught me all about.

If everything in your life is changing, let it.

What I love most about Sundays
is that it never stops
coming around.

Sundays are for slowing down and experiencing
life the way we always should:
with peace and joy, and freedom to do and be what feels
good to us. For centering, for noticing, for beauty, for
gratitude.
For ease.

The Practice of Presence.

Where are you right now? Were you already aware, or did you only stop to think about it because I asked? How often do you stop and think about your presence? How often do you ask yourself questions like:

Am I here, or am I somewhere else? Am I in my body here in the present, or am I in my head somewhere in the past or future?

Practicing presence has enhanced my life in ways I'm still discovering. You know, I just don't want to miss any of it. Life, that is. I don't want to miss something like the stunning, age old trees I pass by on my neighborhood walks. Their roots, inches above the ground, stretched all the way into the neighboring yard. I don't want the years and history that they hold to be lost on me, ever. I want to notice.

And I also want to pay attention to the way I feel and the way I think. And the way things smell, you know? And I want to really taste my food. And I want to be aware of the things I say as well as the words I receive. I want to be fully aware *that I am aware* of what is happening in the now of my life.

Yes, you read that right.

I want to be aware of my awareness.

I want to think to myself, *I am right here, right now*. What is there for me to know or notice in this moment?
There is always something, even if it is just to remember to breathe like I mean it.

I want to be present, here, in my life.

I don't want to miss it at all.

Sunday Affirmations:

Every morning, new mercies I see.

Goodness and mercy follow me, surely.

Every little thing is gonna be alright.

I have so much to look forward to in my life.

I am open.

I am not worried about what I cannot control.

I can trust myself, and that is what I will do.

I surrender again.

It is well.

Everything.

People who are not afraid to reinvent are my kind of people.

I am something brand new as often as I can be.

And I love that for me.

"All The Things" Veggie Soup

What you'll need:*

- 2 tbsp olive oil
  (or your preferred cooking oil)

- 1 large onion, finely chopped

- 3 garlic cloves, minced

- 3 medium carrots, sliced

- 3 celery stalks, chopped

- 1 large sweet potato, peeled and cubed

- 1 bell pepper, chopped
  (color of your choice)

- 1 zucchini, sliced into rounds

- 1 cup green beans, trimmed and cut into bite-sized pieces

- 1 cup diced tomatoes
  (canned or fresh)

- 1 cup chopped kale
  (or spinach)

- 6 cups vegetable broth

- 2-3 fresh sage leaves, finely chopped
  (or 1/2 teaspoon dried sage)

- 1 bay leaf

- Salt and Pepper
  season to taste

* *Really, you can use whatever veggies and spices you have on hand. Have fun and enjoy.*

What you'll do:

1. **Begin with Intention:** Set a soft Sunday tone by gathering your ingredients slowly. As you chop each vegetable, bring a quiet sense of gratitude for its color, shape and the nourishment it offers.

2. **Warm the Pot:** In a large pot, heat the olive oil over medium heat. Add the onion and cook until translucent, about 5 minutes. Add the garlic and cook for another minute, letting the aroma fill the kitchen.

3. **Add Hearty Veggies:** Stir in the carrots, celery, sweet potato and regular potatoes. Sauté gently for 5-7 minutes, allowing the vegetables to start softening and caramelizing slightly.

4. **Layer in Flavors:** Add the bell pepper, zucchini, green beans, diced tomatoes and vegetable broth. Give it a good stir and add the bay leaf and sage. Season with salt and pepper. Cover the pot partially and let the soup simmer for 25-30 minutes, stirring occasionally.

5. **Incorporate the Greens:** After the vegetables are tender, add the kale or spinach. Let the greens wilt into the soup for about 5 minutes. Taste and adjust seasoning if needed.

6. **Serve and Savor:** Ladle the soup into bowls. Sprinkle with fresh parsley, if desired, and enjoy each spoonful slowly, letting the warmth of the soup fill you up from the inside out.

On Sundays we trust that there is always light somewhere. We trust that the sun has not abandoned us. And never will.

Sunday,

Today I don't just need help carrying the load.
Today I need to be the thing that is carried.
Please hold me up. Help my feet to ground so
that I am steady. It feels like I just might fall.
And other times it feels like I want to run.
But to where, Sunday? Where am I supposed to go?
Everywhere hurts. Everywhere seems troubled.

Help me be still, please. Not just my feet, but my mind.
And my racing broken heart.

Help me. Help us. We really need it today –
and every day of this lifetime.

May the grace of Sunday carry and keep you
no matter where you wander.

SUNDAYS IN FALL

Sunday is a good day to focus on the good of your life. Put the rest away for another day.

On Sundays I find some light, no matter how dark.

The Story of Your Life

Could you write a story of your life, and if so how would it read? What genre is your life and who are the main characters besides you? And is your arc morally ascending, descending or staying the same? Or is your life all about transformation? What are the themes? What keeps coming up no matter what you do? What are the big lessons of your life?

I'm asking because I do tend to wonder just how many people are even paying that much attention to their life. It seems as if most people are just going along with it. They are living whatever life happens to them; they are not actively deciding, and they are not intentionally transforming *or* remaining the same. They just so happen to be here. They don't really know which way they're going – and oftentimes they aren't even fully aware of the countless ways they *could* choose to go.

Knowing what to do with life seems quite impossible when we think about what it will all mean in the end, doesn't it? But if we learn to lean into the right now of our life and consider it page by page, just like a story unfolds, our lives are filled with meaning at every turn.

A lot of what I write is for those who are missing their life. I hope they'll see some of my words somewhere somehow and consider paying attention to the next sunset they see. Or the next breath they take.

Take full advantage of the reset Sunday offers.

Do not bring that heaviness over from last week.

It's no longer even real.

You get to let it all go and start fresh.

The only thing that is real is right now.

So.

Unclench your jaw.

Exhale it all.

Inhale this very moment.

You're okay.

Sunday Affirmations:

My life is a miracle.

That thing I feel is true about me – in my core – really is.

I was created with a specific purpose in mind.

I am fulfilling my purpose – even now.

I do not just get by, I thrive.

I am light.

Whatever it is will be okay – better than.

Sundays invite me back inside my body.
They call me to be where I am. Present.
Aware. Feeling. Breathing.
And that's why I love them so.

Back into the light I go.

It's natural to drift.

But.

Back into the light.

Over and again.

On Sunday you can put down the weight
of the past week. You don't have
to carry it anymore.

Giving yourself a break is what *Sunday* feels like.

BRANDIE FREELY

And especially on Sunday morning,
new mercies I can clearly see.

Sunday,

There is nothing quite like you – sweet, soft and slow all at once. Gentle with me, you're like a pool of grace. I love to float in you. And I could stay here forever because of how good you feel on my skin. Like you understand I'll need you consistently, you always come back around. Just when I am depleted. Here you come again with your fullness. You soak into me. And then I am full, too. And I can go on for a little while longer until I need you again... and I certainly will. Because life is not always gentle with me, but you are.

May Sunday bring with it some peace
and some ease.

I need to start over often.
I don't have it all together,
you know?
And that's why I love Sunday.
It feels like a (re)start line.

Sunday Affirmations:

My story is unfolding beautifully.

It always works out for me.

Life is good.

I'm right where I'm supposed to be.

Cheers to more life.

And life more abundantly.

The life I see for myself will be.

I trust time.

May you remember who you are
and may you lift your head.
And may that old, familiar light be there
to shine all over you.
May it feel like it's saying, "Oh, there you are."
And may the corners of your mouth curve upward
as you close your eyes
and release the last of your tears.

The questions are often more important
than the answers.

Author's Note:

The word is curiosity, and it's the tendency to
have good questions about how things work, how they go,
where they come from, and how they can impact you and others.
I think curiosity is actually what gives the cat the nine lives.
You know what I'm saying? Because the more you
come to understand about the world around you,
the more you expand. And become newer versions of yourself.
And create new realities.
New lives for yourself.
You know?
Keep asking the questions, and don't worry so much about the answers.
They change a lot.

Dreamer

I love to dream. Still.

I think it's important to. If we don't dream about the life we really want, then I guess we'll just live whatever life is handed to us? You think that's how it works? I do. A lot of the things that were handed to me (beliefs, customs, ideas) came from places I've never been and people I never even met. I paid enough attention to how those things made me feel to know I didn't want to keep everything, and I eventually learned I didn't have to.

I've been a dreamer for as long as I can remember.
And my dreams have always come true.

I still use my imagination often.
And I really believe in the infinite possibilities of my life.

I really believe, and that
has mattered so much.

Belief is our greatest tool.

May my life be full in every kind of way.
May it have no empty spaces. May it reach
its capacity before it is done. May it
accomplish its mission. May it reach every
place it is meant to go. And may I feel it all
because I am too full not to notice
every little ounce of my life.

Nothing has taken me farther than being open has.

On Sundays I look into how my story is going
and determine whether or not it's in need
of some changes. If so, I simply begin a rewrite.
And I love that for me.

When things are good in your life, let them be. Lean into the good despite whatever is going on around you. Because what if that were the last bit of good you'd ever know? What if your world were to come crashing down tomorrow? Because truth is, it could. *It could*. So lean into whatever good you see or feel or can find. Lean all the way in. While you actually can. You understand?

Sunday feels like a slow and meaningful
exhale after holding your breath at the top.

Author's Note:

Stopping what you're doing to breathe with
intention is a life hack I can't recommend enough.

An easy technique is Box Breathing.

How To:
Inhale for four counts.
Hold that inhale for four counts.
Then slowly exhale for four counts.
Now hold it at the bottom for four counts.
Repeat.

Remind yourself: I am okay right now.

Sundays are for laying my burdens down.

Every crack allows a little light to shine through. Every break opens you up.

Collect Me

Well,
I myself am poetry
Am I not
a word that feels good
falling onto your tongue
Am I not a line you collect
wherever you keep things
with meaning
It feels good
when you remember me, no?
Am I not
finger snapping worthy poetry
And do you not recite me
like you know me well?

Sunday Affirmations:

I am always free to start over.

I can change my whole life starting today if I choose to.

I am very free.

My intentions are very pure and good.

I am a good person.

I can trust that my intuition won't misguide me.

I make good decisions for my life.

I trust myself.

Life is about to get really, really good for me.

The timing is always right.

I haven't seen the best days of my life yet.

I'm getting where I'm going.

Sundays sound like a whisper that says
it's all gonna work out.

Sundays are for moving forward.
Moving on.
Getting over.
Starting fresh.
We can
leave some things in the past,
where they are, which is also
where they belong.

Treat everyday like Sunday, and take good care of yourself.

My goal in life is to master letting it be.

On Sundays, we slow down. We let it be –
whatever it is. We allow our nervous system
to reset and avoid anything that would cause it harm.
We pay attention to our needs on Sundays, and we
cater to ourselves in ways we can't on other days.
That's what we do. *On Sundays.*

How To Keep a Freebird

I say it all the time, because it is true: *I am not easy to keep*. I am all air and wind on the inside. Always dreaming about flying. Always craving to be that high. And that free.

And for a long time I *knew* that about myself, but I wasn't necessarily *okay* with it, because no one else seemed to really be okay with it. You know what I mean? And so I've definitely tried to conform in the past – and in some ways still do – so as not to look crazy for wanting to be so free. Most people don't even understand freedom anyway. To them it's possible I'll always look like a wild woman who couldn't possibly know who she wants to be.

But that's the thing: I know exactly who I want to be. *Who*, you ask?

Well.

I want to be a woman who is free to be whoever I decide I want to be – on *any* given day. I want to be a woman who refuses to stay the same, ever. And I want to be a woman who masters living for herself, first. A woman who is the love of her own life. A woman who knows and has known all about love. Who has lived a life so full, she's overflowing. I want to know all there is to know about what it means to be a woman. You know? I want to be a woman who is in touch with her feelings and her heart – in ways most women aren't. And I want to be a woman who is beautiful from the inside out and filled with an almost ancestral wisdom that beckons other women to sit around, seek answers and hear stories of what it's like to really be free. And I want to be able to paint the most beautiful picture of what freedom looks like, because I have seen it with my own two eyes. I want to have lived so well that I am a beacon of light, an example of how differently you glow when you have felt the world on your skin.

So then, how does one keep a free bird? How would a lover keep a woman like me?

First, he must know that she *is* a free bird long before he ever dares to bring her inside from the wind. He must understand her wings and how they need to fly. He must be careful with her, and treat her as if he knows she is precious and rare. He must love her when she is high up just as much as he longs for her to be grounded and in his arms. He cannot want to hold her more than he wants to see her be herself. He must be willing, even, to be the wind that sustains her at times. He must not wish for her to belong to him, but rather for her to belong to herself.

It must be said that *he, himself*, must be rare. He must know who he is with and without her. And he must not be threatened by her magic. He needs his own kind of magic. The kind that will cause her to want to come inside from the wind where there is comfort and safety and above all, love.

To the one who keeps this free bird, *you are the rarest one.*

On Sunday I'm inspired to try again. To be better this time. To let go of whatever didn't work out. To give myself grace and another chance.

I decided my life is good.

And so it is.

And may Sunday rain some drops of joy down on you. All over your face, turning that frown right side up. May you open your eyes
and see some good somewhere.
It's there. I promise.
Just waiting to be noticed.

Sunday Affirmations:

Life is generous.

I am wide open so I can receive the goodness life wants to offer me.

My heart is healthy and whole.

Love is everywhere. It is abundant.

Life is good.

My mind is well. I am aware of what is real and true.

I love my life and I trust its unfolding.

I am in a perpetual state of bloom.

And it is beautiful. All of it. My whole life's journey.

May you find the courage to fully lean into whatever way your life is currently unfolding.

Harvest

Fall is my favorite romance.
Its themes of flow and surrender
and letting go of what doesn't want
to stay.
And how it is all together so beautiful
even as it changes.
And trusting. And waiting.
And reaping harvest in due time –

are what love look like to me.

Sundays
IN WINTER

Winter is needed because everything has to take its rest. *Everything*. And there is no exception in that. In order for it all to work the way it is designed to, there must be a period of stillness, where everything goes silent for a while. Even the cold and dark are beneficial, because how else would we know how much we love the warmth and light of the sun? It is so important to remember that even in our dormant seasons, life is happening just as it should. Winter is the perfect time to practice trusting time and trusting that the seasons know when to change.

Sunday is a feeling.

Sundays make you feel like everything
is going to be alright. You know?
They just provide this kind of reassurance.
You can't put your finger on it, but you just know.
It's a feeling. A deeply rooted one.

The first sip on a Sunday morning

I like to sip something hot very slowly everyday. But on Sundays, I am especially careful to savor that first sip and pause while it warms my insides. I breathe in, look around at my life – wherever or however it may be – and take it all in. I practice radical acceptance everyday, and especially on Sunday. And the art of deciding, too.

If I look up and see that all is well on Sunday, I quickly decide to allow that to be the story of my life that day. It is well. And I won't consider yesterday or tomorrow, which will only steal some preciousness from the present moment. I just let Sunday be Sunday. Full of ease, sweetness and romance.

And if I look up and see that perhaps there are some things that are not going as well as I'd like on Sunday, I slow my sipping down even further, allowing the heat to soothe my concern on its way down. I close my eyes, exhaling and inhaling deeply, accepting what is and allowing my heart to feel whatever it needs to. Somehow Sunday makes what is heavy a little lighter. It helps me hold it, you know? I just let Sunday be Sunday. A refuge. A salve. A balm.

Sundays are a sweet reminder that we do make it to the other side.
We do.

With Sunday comes some rest and some
relief and some revival.

With Sunday comes a reset. A recharge.
A rebalancing of the mind-body connection.

With Sunday comes simple pleasures and
slowness and sweet surrender.

On Sundays I practice presence. I say to myself, *wherever you are is alright*.

Birdie's Garlic Stuffed Pork Roast

There are some people you meet and immediately know you'll keep forever. It's as if you knew them before – maybe in another lifetime – because your conversation just seems to pick up wherever it left off. That's my Birdie and me. From the very beginning we understood that we spoke the same language, had the same kind of humor, the same view of the world, and both deeply felt the complexities of life and matters of the heart.

Before leaving the south and moving west, I spent many an afternoon in the comfort of Birdie's home, her laughter filling the room and my heart. We'd talk about everything – no topic off limits. And there was this honesty and vulnerability there. It was always warm and sweet. Like the embrace of safe arms.

"You want some of this roast, Brandie?" her southern accent dragging out the first syllable in my name.

"Yes ma'am.
It smells so good."

"Come on, Baby."

Growing up in the south, good food is plentiful. But Birdie's food? Birdie's food is something special. There are two secret ingredients in her food, and I'm going to share them with you.

They are:

Love.
and joy.

She never told me that, but I'm telling you what I know.

And of all the recipes she and countless other southern women who can really cook have shared with me, those two ingredients have made all the difference in my little kitchen.

Birdie would feed me, and then I'd go take an epic nap on her couch. It was a ritual, and I miss it all the time. When I'm homesick, it's for things like an impromptu afternoon with her.

Birdie kept and still keeps a daily journal, and I always loved that about her. I'm pretty sure she mentioned my name on a few pages. And now she knows she's etched on my heart, and in this book forever, too.

What you'll need:

- 1 large pork roast (turkey or beef roast can also be used)
- 1 cup fresh chopped garlic
- 1 small bell pepper, chopped
- 4 medium green and/or red hot peppers, chopped
- 1 small yellow onion, chopped
- 1/4 cup vinegar
- 1/4 cup oil
- Cayenne pepper, salt and black pepper (to taste)

What you'll do:

1. Preheat your oven to 350°F.
2. **Set Your Intention:** Begin by acknowledging the special occasion for which you are preparing this meal. Take a deep breath and appreciate the opportunity to nourish yourself and your loved ones.
3. **Create the Seasoning Blend:** Combine the garlic, bell pepper, hot peppers, onion, vinegar and oil in a bowl. Generously add cayenne pepper, salt and black pepper. Be guided by the ancestors. Mix thoroughly.
4. **Prepare the Roast:**
   - Place the pork roast on a sturdy cutting surface with the bottom side facing up.
   - Using a knife, make angled holes across the bottom of the roast. You can decide if you prefer more holes with lighter seasoning or fewer holes with heavier seasoning. Imagine each hole holding the layers of flavor and love you're infusing into this dish.
   - Carefully stuff each hole with the seasoning mixture.
   - Cut a small piece of meat from the end of the roast and use it to plug the holes. This ensures the seasoning stays in place when the roast is turned over.
5. **Flip and Repeat:** Turn the roast over so the top side is facing up. Create holes on the top but do not stuff them this time.
6. **Prepare the Roaster:** In a heavy roasting pan, add about 1/2 inch of water. Place the roast in the pan. Cover it tightly to lock in moisture.
7. **Roast with Care:**
   - Cook the roast on the bottom rack for 2 1/2 hours, covered.
   - Uncover the roast and continue cooking for another 2 1/2 hours, basting occasionally.
   - Total cooking time: 4-5 hours.
8. **Rest and Reflect:** Once the roast is done, remove it from the oven. Let it rest for a while before slicing. During this time, reflect on the joy of sharing this meal with others.
9. **Serve with Love:** This roast is best enjoyed alongside comforting sides such as:
   - White rice or broccoli rice
   - Green beans
   - Greens (mustards or collards)
   - Cabbage
   - Yams
   - Mac and cheese from scratch
   - Sweet peas with lots of butter and a touch of sugar
   - Glazed carrots with a dash of ginger, butter and a little sugar

Sunday Nap:

(n.) a deep, short sleep that heals and restores.

Deep down we all know what's best for us. If we don't know, we haven't gone deep enough.

On Sundays I do the work to keep my mind.
The work is rest.

May the spirit of Sunday get inside your
bones and hold you together all week long.
May it be like a gentle wind that lifts you up
and carries you wherever you're going.
May you float along until you arrive once again
safely, at Sunday.

Sunday Affirmations:

I can do hard things.

I invite ease into every situation – even hard ones.

I was created for and am equipped to follow my dreams.

The Master Creator, God, loves when I create.

My imagination is worth preserving.

I am allowed to think and exist outside the box.

My dreams are for real.

I can decide the life I live.

Miracles are for real.

My very life is a miracle.

I am light.

I am electric.

Wherever I am is a little less dark than it was before I arrived.

What If

it's all gonna happen exactly one
year from now. What if the dream
you've been dreaming or working
towards is going to all come together
and work out in your favor on this
very day, next year. What if you get a
call that the answer is finally yes
just one year from today. And all you have to do
right now
is just do everything you can to trust the timing
of your life until then.
And keep showing up for yourself
until then.
And keep believing it's possible until then.

What if it's gonna take another year –
or even two – to happen, and you won't have any proof at all.

Can you be patient and still trust the timing of your life?

Because although you can't see it now,
the dream is certainly coming together.

May I be the woman of my own dreams first and foremost.

Celebrate yourself.
Exhale –

Everything it took to be
right where you are.
Only you know.

Eyes closed.
Deep inhale.

You made it.
And that's no small thing.
No small thing at all.

No, seriously. Make it a habit to take good care on Sundays. Or whatever day feels right to you. The habit of checking in with yourself is the most important part. You know?

Author's Note:

Sometimes your *Sunday* is on a *Saturday*.
Your sabbath. Your sacred, intentional rest.
And that's okay.
That's perfectly okay, too.

Sunday,

You were made for me, and I you. We just get one another, don't we? We're so much alike. Both easy. Both intentional. Both full of loveliness. Both desiring to slow the things around us down. Both in love with rest. Both in love with doing whatever feels right and good and soft and sweet. We both love the idea of surrender, don't we. *Sunday, are we best friends?* I love you so much, and I love when you come around. You remind me of myself. You know? And I need that reminder so often. Thank you, Sunday. I'm forever yours.

May I trust this part of myself.
And know. That wherever I am right here, right now —
is the entry point to wherever I'm going
and am supposed to be. And
is the single most significant part of my journey so far.
Yes. This moment. Where I am right now.

Breathe here.

May I treasure it as such.
May I learn to love and lean into the now.
May the practice of being where I am grow stronger
and stronger. And stronger.
That I might surrender again. And again.
Remembering that all I really have is the precious
moment I'm in.
Past gone.
Future unknown.

It's just me and right now.
And it's beautiful.
Because I decided so.

Whatever

is heavy

lay

it

down.

The hardest part is not *knowing* what to do but
doing what we know.

Sunday Affirmations:

Whatever I think I need, I already have within me.

I am covered.

My life is precious and valuable. More than I can even comprehend.

I am leaning into the now.

I trust that everything happening in my life is happening for my good.

When it's all said and done, it will all make sense.

I release what I can't control. Right now.

I surrender.

Experience

Shedding,
she is
removing layers
dried up by years
and time
and journey
to
uncover
the newness that wishes
to be revealed
underneath
all the life
that has
been lived
there is still more life
to *feel*
on her skin
so she can be sure
it's real.

God – thank You for everyday, but especially
Sunday. Because on Sunday the world slows down enough for me to actually feel you breathe new life into me. And there's
nothing I want more.

Letter to my fourteen year old daughter and my fourteen year old self:

I wish you could see yourself the way I do. You're as close to perfect as anyone could possibly be. Absolutely beautiful just how you are. You don't need to be like anyone except yourself. I know it feels like being more like *that* person, or *her over there*, would mean that *maybe* more people would love you. And I know what it is to just wanna be loved. *I do.* But listen to your mommy: You are so lovable. You've always been. You're my dream girl; the one I always wanted. And when I look at you I think, *if only you knew how special you are.* And *if only you could see* how beautifully your life will unfold if you'll just give it time.

Everything grows and blooms and becomes – if you'll just allow for time and water and soil and sun to do their thing.

Four things I want you to know:

time – patience and trust
water – what helps you grow
soil – the whole of the human experience
sun – finding a way to find the light

> ***Four other things:***
>
> spring – all things made like new
> summer – we bask in the warmth of the sun and enJOY
> fall – we allow things to change
> winter – we accept endings and allow our hearts and minds to rest

continued...

For everything, there is a season. PawPaw would let you know those words are written in Ecclesiastes 3:1-8 in the good book.

And I will tell you that what it says is so true. Every single thing has its proper time, *and* if we can learn to trust that time is always on our side – because it always is – we can unlock a new level of living that only few get to experience.

I hope you believe me when I tell you that one day you'll grow up and all these fourteen year old things will feel so small in comparison to the expansive life you'll get to live. You'll come to understand that at fourteen you're just now beginning to figure out who you might want to be.

You'll change your mind so many times from here until you're as old as your mommy. And that's perfectly okay.

You are always free to change your mind.

I hope you believe me when I
tell you your life will become
so wonder-*full*. And hear me:
there's no need to rush it. All
you need to do is let it. I know
you want a first crush and a
first kiss. *I know you do*, and
I understand. I want it for
you, too. It'll happen. You'll
experience love in so many
ways. Ways you don't even yet
know exist. Take your time. You
don't have to rush a thing, and
I pray you never let anyone rush
you.

You are free to take all of your precious time.

You'll remember fourteen for
how it felt, so be careful with
your *feelings* and remember
they are not *facts*. Don't hold on
so tightly to them. Don't find
your life's truth in them. *You
hear me?*

*You are so much more than you even yet
know.*
I wish you could see yourself the way I do.
How beautiful you are.
How brilliant.
How set apart you are from the rest.

                                                                            I see you.
And I am so proud of you,
you very special girl.

I am what I need.

SUNDAYS IN WINTER

Sundays are for moments of gentle doing.
And mostly *being*.

On Sundays we make feeling good the priority.

On Sundays, I only want to be soft and do soft things.

Sunday,

I'm so glad I can count on you. Because sometimes I just need to start over, and not everyone gets that like you do. I can come to you just like I am, un-put-together, and you never mind. You don't make me feel less than. You simply shine your loving light on me and help me see who I really am. I wish everyday felt like you, but then maybe I wouldn't cherish you enough. I don't know. I feel like I still would. You're just far too good, too wonder-full not to adore.

Sunday Affirmations:

It is well. All of it.

Today is the start of a beautiful new week.

I am blessed and kept.

It is working together for me.

I will trust the process.

I will notice the good all around me.

I will stay in the light.

I can always begin again.

On Sundays, we take breathing seriously.
Heart at a resting rate. We take it easy.
We breathe deeply and with intention.
We check our pulse. Our internal temperature.
We do our maintenance.
On Sundays, we don't take being alive lightly
at all.

And when you drift too far, may you remember that you can always find your anchor on Sunday.

Our Default.

Things I think about while showering or talking to myself in the car.

It occurred to me the other day that we have default settings. Each of us. These default settings have a lot to do with our formation. They have a lot to do with things we've believed (whether true or not) for a large part of our lives. These defaults are what many of us will spend a lot of time unlearning as we grow older. We will come to understand that the defaults are a part of other people's programming. Other people's systems. Other people's truths and beliefs that were then passed down to us. They never *really* belonged to us, these defaults.

Yet we can't help but operate in them – unless we really do the work of not allowing ourselves to. And that can be hard.

What are some of your defaults? Your mode of operandi. Your patterns.

I think one way to identify them is by recognizing what you do when you're *not* at your best. When things aren't going as well as you'd like. I think *that* is when we go back to default. You know what I mean? When things are great, we practice the unlearning and we implement our new, more enlightened systems. Don't we? And we feel ourselves making progress and becoming better. And it's beautiful. Until we hit an *ebb*, and our *flow* stops.

Then here come those default ways, behaviors, systems.

All unlearning forgotten.

I like using the term default, because we know and understand that the default is always there. At the click of a button, things can always go back to the way they were. Our minds understand system updates and upgrades. We understand the need for maintenance to keep our systems optimized. Don't we?

And that's why on Sundays we do maintenance on our systems. Our nervous systems. We identify which parts of us are operating in default settings. We update. We reset. We shut down. And let the whole thing rest. Let it process.

Let it slowly restart.

Just get me to Sunday.

SUNDAYS IN WINTER

Sundays have long been the place we lay our burdens down.
We rest. We do the things that make us feel light
in a dark and heavy world. We've loved Sundays
for a long time, and they have loved us back so well.

Sunday Affirmations:

I have the most control when I surrender all.

I don't need to know everything for everything to work together for me.

My name is being spoken highly of in rooms I'm not even aware exist.

Doors are opening for me.

I am prepared to walk into places and spaces God intended for me to be in.

It's only up from here.

I'm entering a really, really good part.

Life is good to me.

Life is generous.

Life is kind.

And everyday I am learning and practicing how to best surrender to it.

Sundays are for coming back to my center.

My Favorite Cream Cheese Pound Cake

What you'll need:

- 3 cups all purpose flour
- 1 teaspoon baking powder
- 1/4 teaspoon baking soda
- 1/2 teaspoon salt
- 1 1/2 cups salted butter (Room Temperature)
- 1 8oz package cream cheese (Room Temperature)
- 6 large eggs (Room Temperature)
- 2 3/4 cups granulated white sugar
- 2 1/2 teaspoons pure vanilla
- Zest of a lemon

What you'll do:

1. **Prepare to Bake:** Preheat your oven to 325°F. Grease and flour a 10-inch bundt pan.*
2. **Gather Ingredients:** Lay out all your ingredients. This helps make your process more enjoyable.
3. **Cream Butter and Cream Cheese:** In a large mixing bowl, beat the butter and cream cheese together on medium speed until smooth and creamy (about 2-3 minutes). Pause and notice the silky texture.
4. **Add Sugar Gradually:** Slowly add sugar, 1/2 cup at a time, beating well after each addition. Notice how the mixture becomes fluffy and light – let this symbolize how you're creating something beautiful from simple ingredients.
5. **Incorporate Eggs One by One:** Add eggs, one at a time, mixing just until combined. Observe how the batter changes with each egg, becoming richer.

* *I like to use the paper from the butter and rub it around the pan once I've added the sticks to my large bowl for mixing.*

6. **Add Vanilla:** Stir in the vanilla extract. Take a moment to breathe in the warm, inviting aroma.

7. **Sift and Add Flour:** In a separate bowl, sift together all the dry ingredients. Slowly add this to the wet ingredients, mixing on low speed until just combined. Avoid overmixing.

8. **Pour and Smooth:** Pour the batter into your buttered pan. Smooth the top with a spatula, appreciating the glossy, thick batter.

9. **Bake with Presence:** Place the cake in the oven. Bake for 75-90 minutes, or until a toothpick inserted into the center comes out clean. As the cake bakes, enjoy the scent that fills your kitchen – it's a reminder to savor life's sweetness.

10. **Let Cool:** Let the cake cool in the pan for 10-15 minutes before turning it out onto a wire rack. Place your hand on the pan, feeling its warmth as the cake releases.

11. **Optional Glaze:** If you wish, whisk powdered sugar, milk or cream, vanilla and juice from your lemon in a small bowl until smooth. Drizzle over the cooled cake, letting it cascade naturally.

Serve with Intention:

Slice the cake gently, taking in its soft crumb and creamy texture. Serve it on your favorite plate, and enjoy with a warm drink. Notice every bite – the sweetness, the hint of vanilla, the slight tang from the cream cheese. Reflect on the care and presence that went into creating this treat.

BRANDIE FREELY

As it turns out, Sundays
are a good day historically.

Author's Note:

I grew up in church. Southern Baptist to
be exact. The Pastor's Daughter. The singing kind.
My roots are deep and so is my reverence for the
sacredness of Sunday. I am not the first nor
the last to favor this day out of all the others
in the week. People have looked forward to the
spiritual recharge of Sunday since before mine
and my mama's and her mama's time.
Sundays have always meant something to us.
They've carried us, really.
They have kept us.
Amen.

May you give yourself time and grace
to get it all together.

Sundays feel a lot like returning home.

Sundays are for surrendering.
Again.

Sunday,

Open me up. Soften me. Help me breathe with more intention
and purpose and gratitude flowing in and out of me.
Give me renewed strength. A second wind
to keep keeping on. Give me sight to see where I'm going.
Clarity about the days and weeks ahead.
Restore whatever hope I lost last week for whatever reasons.
Remind me that I can start over right here right now.
Be sweet to me, Sunday. I need it. And I know you have a lot of
sweetness to give.

Sunday Affirmations:

I am free to feel how I feel.

I am free to express those feelings or not.

I am allowed to be unsure sometimes.

I am allowed to retreat from it all to sit with my thoughts.

I don't have to have all the right answers all the time.

I do know some things for sure (even when my mind is full of questions):

I am loved.

      I am seen.

           I am known.

                  I am kept.

                        It is well.

And alas, on Sunday
I can get somewhere
and find some stillness.

Thing is,
anytime I've ever
made it to the other
side of anything,
the grass has always
been greener.

Piecing It Together

Right now I'm in East Texas on the ranch my parents just purchased for our family.

I absolutely love it here.

Thirty eight acres of fifty-foot pine trees and about thirty magnificent Magnolia trees hidden throughout. Magnolias are my favorite, so unexpectedly finding them all over the property felt like a Godwink saying *welcome home*.

And it's so interesting, because my *mama's* mama was born not too far from here in a small town called Camden. And *then*, there's this Native American reservation about twenty minutes up the road, right? Well. We are descendents on my dad's side. Isn't it absolutely wild that we would end up on this land?

Maybe that has something to do with why I feel so good here. Like I've known every inch of this place all my life. I'm comfortable in every corner. And you'd *think* all these trees and piercing silence might be a bit unnerving, you know? But no, it's actually the most peaceful thing. Everything inside me feels properly regulated in the stillness.

continued...

There are two really large ponds on our land. One holds a good amount of nice sized catfish, which my uncle (daddy's baby brother) has forbidden anyone to be *out there catchin' all willy-nilly*. The other pond has a really cool little boat house on a large dock and bass that are good for the catching.

I see myself spending a lot of time here. I already have my heart set on building a beautiful home deep in the woods behind the smaller pond. I'd love a chicken coup for fresh eggs in the mornings. And multiple gardens. Vegetables. Fruit. Flowers that I'll pick for a fresh bouquet on Sundays. Maybe a small greenhouse for rares and evergreens and expensive, exotic plants that require a special skill set to be kept alive, *you know*, extra care to be kept alive. I'd love to have a couple of horses one day. I'd love to learn to ride and care for them. *Or maybe I'll have someone help with that part. We'll see.*

I'm pretty sure I'll host retreats here. It is perfect for an escape. There's a wide, wooden porch that wraps around the front of the house and around to a gorgeous pool out back. I've spent a lot of time there, rocking back and forth while piecing the final pages of this book together.

I've been waking up before the sun and waiting for it to peek through the trees so I have just enough light to go out. I am a true outdoorsy person. What about you? I mean, so long as it's some kind of pretty – the type of landscape doesn't matter – I can stay outside from sunup to sundown. It's my preference. And if I must be inside, hopefully the windows are just about as large as life, allowing some good light to come in.

Everything I'm telling you? I get to tell you, and imagine it at all, because of my daddy. My daddy is the greatest visionary I know. I'm certain everything in me that knows how to make my dreams real comes from him. He did the very best with what he had, and it became generational. That was his dream in life: *to leave his children's children's children with something*. And he did. He has.

continued...

I'm currently sitting with him in a small room just to the left of the front door. He's sitting in the seat built into his walker, staring out of a floor to ceiling window. It's stunning. We're both still so taken with this scenery and the fact that it's ours. We sit in silence for a while, and then to break it and connect a little, I say, "I'm writing a book called *Sundays + Other Musings*."

I tell him a bit about its premise. He listens but doesn't respond. Just continues staring out the window.

Daddy will likely never read this book. And he'll never ask questions about it, like where the idea came from or why I chose to create a collection of words around Sundays.

He may pick it up and admire it. Maybe he'll flip through the pages when I'm not around.

He may even tell his friends about it. They're all getting up in age now, and some have passed on. I'm sure he'll tell them, *this is Brandie's new book*. And go on and on about the things I'm doing in the world. *He knows because he listens in when I'm on the phone with my mama.*

Everything I'm telling you? I'm telling you because I want you to see what radical acceptance looks like. I am not disappointed that my daddy will likely never read this book. Instead, I am grateful that his life and example led me here. To this collection of Sunday words and prayers. To being the visionary I am. To believing my dreams can be real. To loving people. To God. To holding space for people and encouraging them. And being a light. And a vessel.

You see, I am definitely my mother's daughter. And while I may not be the kind of daddy's girl you see on tv or read about, I am most certainly also his.

I asked him just now, "Daddy. You wanna add anything to my book? What would you say about Sundays?"

He waves his hand and shakes his head, his once broad and strong shoulders slouched forward on the handles of his walker.

"What about a scripture or song?"

He begins to sing:

Guide me, O Thou great Jehovah,
Pilgrim through this barren land.
I am weak, but Thou art mighty;
Hold me with Thy powerful hand...

Acknowledgments

There are people in my life who honestly believe in me more than I do. At various stops along my journey, they have been there. Life giving, they have been, providing fuel for the road ahead. I don't know where these people come from or why I was chosen to know them, but I'm so glad my path intersected with each of theirs. And I want to acknowledge them now. You know who you are. You see me. You know me. You've always believed there is a purpose and a plan beyond whatever we could see. Even when I found it hard to. You've believed for me. And it has meant the world just to know you. And to have you as a friend.

It's also so important that I acknowledge the many people I've not yet had the pleasure of meeting in person. But who support me anyway. Who send me love and affirmations on a daily basis and give me reason to keep going. It was you who sent messages encouraging me to put these words in a book, because you wanted something pretty for your coffee tables and bookshelves. Your big love over the years has allowed me to live the life of my dreams, really. And. It has given me reason to keep dreaming. Even bigger. And bigger still.

Thank you is far too small, but.

I *sincerely* thank you.

Finally, it must be said, this book could not exist in this way without my designer, editor, sometimes co-writer and friend, Emily. I hope you feel as special as you truly are. You're a true Godsend in my life, and I'd have a stack of incomplete projects without you.

About the Author

For over two decades, Brandie Freely has been a guiding light for women seeking profound personal transformation. As a sought-after wellness educator, retreat host and facilitator, and published author, she creates sacred spaces where women explore their inner wisdom and step into lives of purpose and authenticity.

Brandie's written works have touched thousands and include: *Sundays + Other Musings*, *truths. and freedoms.* and the *Self-Study Journal.* They each offer readers intimate pathways to self-discovery and healing. As the Editor-in-Chief of Lumin Magazine, she explores how creativity and well-being intersect in the lives and stories of people of color.

A Texas native, Brandie currently resides in Long Beach, California with her family.

Find Brandie and more of her work on brandiefreely.com and @brandiefreely on social media.